CW00662816

HONEY is the matchless, natural,
and non-fattening food for long-life,
virility, and mental alertness ...

THE MAGIC OF HONEY
COOKBOOK

is full of delectable recipes every one
utilising the taste and goodness
contained in honey *and* each recipe
has been tried and tested in Barbara
Cartland's own kitchen.

Also by Barbara Cartland

BOOKS OF LOVE, LIFE AND HEALTH
THE YOUTH SECRET
THE FASCINATING FORTIES
MEN ARE WONDERFUL
FOOD FOR LOVE
LOVE, LIFE AND SEX

HISTORICAL BIOGRAPHY
THE OUTRAGEOUS QUEEN
THE PRIVATE LIFE OF CHARLES II
THE SCANDALOUS LIFE OF KING CAROL
DIANE DE POITIERS
METTERNICH

ROMANCES
THE MAGNIFICENT MARRIAGE
THE KARMA OF LOVE
THE MASK OF LOVE
A SWORD TO THE HEART
BEWITCHED
THE IMPETUOUS DUCHESS
SHADOW OF SIN
GLITTERING LIGHTS
THE DEVIL IN LOVE
THE TEARS OF LOVE

and published by Corgi Books

Barbara Cartland

The Magic of
Honey Cookbook

CORGI BOOKS
A DIVISION OF TRANSWORLD PUBLISHERS LTD

THE MAGIC OF HONEY COOKBOOK

A CORGI BOOK 0 552 10066 8

First publication in Great Britain

PRINTING HISTORY
Corgi edition published 1976
Copyright © Barbara Cartland 1976

Corgi Books are published by
Transworld Publishers Ltd.,
Century House, 61–63 Uxbridge Road,
Ealing, London W5 5SA
Made and printed in Great Britain by
Cox & Wyman Ltd., London, Reading and Fakenham

Editor of:
The Common Problems by Ronald Cartland (with a preface by the
Rt. Hon. The Earl of Selborne, P.C.)

Drama:
Blood Money
French Dressing

Philosophy:
Touch the Stars

Radio Operetta;
The Rose and the Violet (Music by Mark Lubbock) performed in 1942.

Radio Plays:
The Caged Bird: An episode in the life of Elizabeth, Empress of
Austria. Performed in 1957.

Verse:
Lines on Life and Love.

CONTENTS

Foreword
by
Barbara Cartland

As the Magic of Honey has now become a world bestseller I have been asked to write down some of the dishes made with Honey which we eat ourselves.

The great Honey producing countries of the world have given me their special recipes and my chef Nigel Gordon has tried them all out in my kitchen.

When I was writing the Magic of Honey I learnt that Dr. A. P. Bentall, Senior Consultant Gynaecologist and Obstetrician at the Norfolk and Norwich hospital always uses liquid Honey on open wounds. He told me that it is less toxic, contains more vitamins, heals quickly and is better for the patient than anything else.

It is obvious therefore that if Honey can heal an open wound, it will heal the wind pipe through which we breathe and live. It will also heal all through the body.

I believe that Honey given by God is the greatest medicine, the strongest energiser and stimulator in the world. It is important for sex, for a balanced mind, and a happy intellect.

In fact Mohammed was right when he said, "Honey is the medicine of the East."

In compiling this book I am most grateful to
Monsieur Paul Haeberlin of the Auberge de l'Illhäusern, France.

9

The Australian Overseas Trade Office and Barker Newslines.

The Austrian Embassy.

Herr R. Schmitz, Manager of the Brenners Park Hotel in Baden-Baden.

The Canadian High Commissioner and the Canadian Department of Agriculture.

Her Excellency Mrs. Claire Broumas of the Greek Embassy.

Miss Christine Campbell of The Honey Bureau, 15 Thayer Street, London, W.1.

Mrs. Fanny Cradock.

S. A. Lagden Esq. of Kimpton Bros. Ltd., 2 Chandos Street, London, W1M 0EH—the major Honey Importers in the United Kingdom.

Patrick Forbes of Moet and Chandon (London) Ltd.

Ted Maloney.

The Embassy of the U.S.A. and the American Embassy Women's Association.

I believe this book will bring on both health and happiness – because there is magic in it.

FISH DISHES

Fish Kebabs	12
Spicy Prawn Salad with Sauce	13
Spicy Sauce	14
Sweet Fish	14
Trout in Honey	15

Fish Kebabs

from Gales Honey Bureau

Ingredients:

     2 lbs. Cod
     2 Small Onions
     2 tblsps. Oil
     3 tblsps. Wine Vinegar
     4 tblsps. Honey
     1 tblsp. Lemon Juice
     1 teasp. Mixed Herbs
     1 tblsp. Parsley
     Pinch of Salt.

Method: Cut the cod into cubes. Peel the onions and cut into quarters and then separate into pieces. Thread the pieces of fish on to 4 skewers, alternating with pieces of onion. Place all the other ingredients in a bowl and mix together and season with salt and pepper. Lay the fish skewers in a shallow baking tray and pour over the marinade. Leave covered, in a cool place for two hours. Cook under a moderate grill, basting frequently with the remainder of the marinade.

Nigel Gordon: Serve on a bed of rice and with a lettuce salad.

Barbara Cartland: Everyone who has ever studied the history of Honey is convinced that it has a magic ingredient. Although Honey has been analysed for hundreds of years by scientists of every generation, there remains a mysterious 4 per cent which they have never been able to break down.

Spicy Prawn Salad with Sauce

from Gales Honey Bureau

Ingredients:

> 12 Radishes
> 4 oz. Peas
> 6 Carrots
> 4 ozs. Prawns
> 1 Cos Lettuce

Method: Slice the radishes. Cut the carrots into fine strips. Wash the lettuce. Place all the salad ingredients and most of the prawns in layers in individual glasses. Decorate with the rest of the prawns or for a special treat, use tinned, peeled King prawns.

Spicy Sauce

Ingredients:

> 2 tblsps. Clear Honey
> Squeeze Lemon Juice
> 1 teasp. Wine Vinegar
> 2 Drops Soy Sauce
> Pinch Mixed Spice
> Pinch Dry Mustard

Method: Shake all the ingredients together and pour over the salads just before serving.

Nigel Gordon: This is a good starter for a dinner party and not too filling.

Barbara Cartland: Honey contains the minerals and the very important vitamins which are absolutely essential to life. These are also found in other products, but in Honey there is I believe the Elixir of Life. This is why Honey is stimulating to Sex and has fantastic healing properties.

Sweet Fish

from Gales Honey Bureau

Ingredients:

> 4 Whole Boned Herrings
> 2 Green Eating Apples
> 2 Small Onions

2 tblsps. Honey
1 oz. Butter
2 teasps. Mixed Herbs

Method: Place the herrings in a buttered oven dish and arrange the apples, which have been cored and sliced, and thinly sliced onions on top. Sprinkle with a little lemon juice. Heat the butter, honey and herbs over a low heat until the honey dissolves. Pour over the fish, and cover with a buttered paper and bake for 20 minutes at 375°F, Mark 5.

Nigel Gordon: You can leave this dish to get cold, then roll the herrings and serve with a mustard sauce. This way you will have the sweet fish and the biting taste of the mustard sauce together.

Barbara Cartland: When the ancient Phoenician traders came to Britain in search of tin and lead, they found such enormous quantities of Honey they called Britain "The Isle of Honey"! The Druids called us "The Honey Isle of Beli".

Trout in Honey

Ingredients:

2 Trout
2 Onions
2 teasps. Honey
1 tblsp. Oil

4 Mushrooms
½ glass White Wine
1 tblsp. Chopped Parsley
1 teasp. Caraway Seeds
½ teasp. Chili Sauce
Salt and Pepper

Nigel Gordon: Chop the onions and mushrooms, put in a long dish and add honey, wine, oil, caraway seeds, parsley, chili sauce, salt and pepper. Put in the fish, cover and leave to marinate for half an hour. Gently cook the fish in the marinade on top of the stove until done. Remove the fish and serve with a butter sauce.

Barbara Cartland: When the Romans landed in Britain they found that everyone ate Honey with the result that all the Britains were very strong and beautiful.

One historian wrote "These Britains only begin to grow old at 120."

Another wrote "These islanders consume large quantities of Honey-brew (or Mead)".

CHICKEN, GAME AND DUCK DISHES

Chicken, Honey and Oranges

from American Embassy Wives' Association

Ingredients:

> 1 3 lb. Chicken
> ½ cup Butter
> ¼ cup Flour
> 1 teasp. Salt
> 2 teasps. Paprika
> ¼ teasp. Pepper
> 2 tblsps. Honey
> ½ teasp. Ginger
> 1½ cups Orange Juice
> 1½ cups Water
> 1 teasp. Tabasco Sauce
> 2 Oranges

Method: Sprinkle chicken with salt, pepper, paprika and brown in butter. Remove chicken and stir into the casserole the flour, honey, tabasco, ginger, orange juice and water. Return chicken to the sauce, cover and cook until chicken is tender. Slice oranges ½ inch thick and add to chicken. Cook for a short while longer then serve.

Nigel Gordon: This is a very unusual dish and the orange gives it a very nice flavour.

Barbara Cartland: Mead in some form has been brewed by primitive tribes all over the world from India to Lithuania and always contained Honey.

Ancient Greeks called their Honey-wine *Hydromel* and believed it would disperse anger, sweep away sadness and affliction of the mind and make those who drank it warm and lovely. This is why Honey has always been called "The Food of Love".

Chicken with Almond Honey

from New Zealand

Ingredients:

>1 Boiling Fowl
>3 ozs. Butter
>3 ozs. Blanched Almonds
>4 tblsps. Honey

Method: Boil the chicken and remove meat in large pieces. Melt butter, chop and add almonds, honey and a little chicken stock and simmer over a low heat until thick. Coat the chicken pieces with the sauce.

Nigel Gordon: For decoration add a little chopped red pepper. Serve with rice.

Barbara Cartland: Rudolf Steiner discovered the amazing harmony and happiness existing in a beehive. "The whole hive," he wrote, "is in reality permeated with love . . . the bee lives in an atmosphere completely pervaded by love." He also said, "Nothing is better for man than to add the right proportion of Honey to his food".

Chicken in the Gold

from: Sri Lanka

Ingredients:

2 1½ lb. Chickens
4 ozs. Golden Honey
2 dstsps. Curry Powder
1 Beaten Egg
2 dstsps. Mustard Powder
1 oz. Melted Butter
Pepper and Salt

Method: Wash chicken and cut into slices, dry on a cloth. Mix together salt, pepper and curry powder. Season chickens well with this by rubbing into them.

Mix together beaten egg and mustard and then add butter. Brush well on all the pieces of chicken and grill skin side up. Turn about every five minutes. Baste with the honey mixture. Cook for about 30 minutes or until done. Serve hot.

Nigel Gordon: Serve the chicken with fried onion rings, hard boiled eggs and celery curls. A good sauce with this dish is ½ oz. butter, 1 tblsp. flour, ¼ pint cream, ¼ pint milk, plus honey and curry powder to flavour.

Barbara Cartland: The warm, moist climate in Sri Lanka gives the women a clear, flawless skin. They never have lines or wrinkles however old they grow. We now have in the Health Stores the magical Propolis which was known to the ancient Greeks. It is the substance with which the bees seal their combs and exclude all bacteria. Propolis heals ulcers and gastric upsets, magics away a sore throat and cures acne quicker than any other product in existence.

Duck with Orange Sauce

Ingredients:

> 1 3 lb. Duck
> 1 oz. Sugar
> 1 tblsp. Vinegar
> 2 Oranges
> $\frac{1}{4}$ pint Meat Stock
> Pinch Arrowroot
> 1 tblsp. Honey
> $\frac{1}{2}$ teasp. Lemon Juice
> Chopped Orange Peel

Nigel Gordon: Roast the duck in a hot oven 400°F, Mark 7 until done. Remove breast and cut into thin slices. Cook the remainder of the duck with the meat stock until fairly strong. Strain and thicken with arrowroot. Brown the sugar in a thick-bottomed pan and dissolve in the vinegar. Beat up in the liquid, the honey, the juice of the oranges and half the lemon, and the orange peel. Bring to the boil and pour over the breast of the duck.

Barbara Cartland: In Tudor days the robust, adventurous, strong Britons all ate Honey. But Queen Elizabeth got a liking for the sugar called the Honey Bearing-Reed, which was brought home from the West Indies by her ships. She used to gorge herself on it, unlike the common Honey eaten by her poorer subjects. It caused her teeth to decay and go black.

Honeyed Chicken

from Australia

Ingredients:

> 3 lbs. Chicken
> 3 ozs. Butter
> 4 Shallots
> ½ cup Dry Sherry
> 1 teasp. Finely Chopped Green Ginger
> 1 tblsp. Honey
> 1 tblsp. Soy Sauce
> ½ teasp. Salt and Pepper

Method: Melt the butter in a baking dish and place the well-seasoned chicken in it basting it with the melted butter. Roast in a moderate oven 350°F, Mark 4 for 45 minutes basting from time to time. Finely chop the onions and mix with the sherry, ginger, honey, soy sauce, salt and pepper and pour it over the chicken.

Go on roasting for another 30 minutes or until the chicken is tender and golden brown, basting it frequently with the sauce.

Nigel Gordon: This chicken has a ginger flavour through it which makes it a very nice and flavourable dish.

Barbara Cartland: The athletes of Ancient Greece were all trained on Honey and they found that a drink of Honey and water quickly banished fatigue. Many of them believed Honey would prolong life and endow them with perpetual youth.

Honeyed Chicken

from Greece

Ingredients:

> 2 3 lb. Chickens
> 1 cup Honey
> 1½ cups Wheat Germ
> 1 tblsp. Chopped Parsley
> ½ teasp. Thyme
> ½ teasp. Basil
> Salt and Pepper
> Soy Oil

Method: Cut chicken into serving pieces and dip in honey for a thin coating. Mix together the wheat-germ, parsley, thyme, basil, salt and pepper. Coat honeyed chicken with wheat-germ mixture. Add soy oil to depth of ½ inch in a heavy skillet and heat. Add chicken pieces in a single layer and cook over medium to low heat until brown. Turn the pieces several times. Cover skillet and cook until chicken is done, approx. 15 minutes.

Nigel Gordon: This is a very tasty and healthy dish, all made with natural foods.

Barbara Cartland: The Middle East has always laid great store by Honey and believed that it helped those who ate it to obtain eternal life. Mohammed said "Honey is the medicine of the Soul, benefit yourselves by the use of the Koran and Honey!"

Honeyed Turkey

from Gales Honey Bureau

Ingredients:

> 1 6 lb. Turkey
> 12 Large Prunes
> 12 Walnuts
> 1 lb. Pork Sausage-meat
> 1 med. Onion
> 3 tblsps. Honey
> 1 Egg

Method: Place the onion, sausage-meat and egg in a bowl and mix thoroughly. Stone the prunes, which have been soaked overnight, and fill with the walnut pieces. Dip the filled prunes in honey and put in the sausage-

24

meat mixture. Pack the stuffing into the bird and wrap in double thickness foil. Put in the middle of a pre-heated oven 325°F, Mark 3 and roast for 3 hours. Halfway through cooking open the foil, baste the turkey in its own juices and pour over it 3 tblsps. Honey. Re-close the foil. For a very crisp skin open the foil for the last 20 minutes of cooking.

Nigel Gordon: The turkey can be roasted on its side and turned half way or laid on its breast which ensures that the breast will stay moist.

Barbara Cartland: In the past, Egyptian Bridegrooms were expected to supply their brides with Honey. At the marriage ceremony the groom promised his wife 24 *hins* of Honey which was about 32 lbs.

Peking Duck

from Mrs. Fanny Cradock

Ingredients:

1 Plump Duck
1 cup Thin Honey
Salt
Milled Black Peppercorns

Method: Hang the duck by its feet in a draught for twenty-four hours. Rub all over with salt and pepper. Then take two table forks and prick the bird all over. Place the duck on an ordinary wine rack, stand both in a meat baking-tin and smear the thin honey all over the bird. Place the duck in the middle of the oven 375°F, Mark 5 and allow to cook for 40 minutes. Pour away the duck fat which has accumulated in the pan. Return to oven and continue roasting for 60 minutes more.

Nigel Gordon: When the duck is ready the skin should be crisp, succulent and the colour of an unpeeled chestnut.

Barbara Cartland: The Brahmins of Bengal anointed the Indian forehead, lips, eyelids, and ear lobes with Honey to ward off evil spirits and make certain of a happy marriage. In some Far Eastern races the bride would be anointed with Honey on her breasts and private regions to ensure fertility.

Roast Duck with Apple Stuffing

from Gales Honey Bureau

Ingredients:

1 5 lb. Duck
6 slices Granary Bread
1 lb. Cooking Apples
1 Medium Onion
1 teasp. Mixed Herbs
1 tblsp. Dry Sherry
2 tblsps. Honey
1 oz. Walnuts

Method: Remove the crusts from the bread and crumble into large pieces. Peel the apples and onion and chop finely. Combine with the bread. Add the other ingredients and mix well together. Stuff the Duck. Rub the outside of the duck with salt and pepper and roast at 425°F, Mark 7, for 15 minutes and then at 375°F, Mark 5 allowing 15 minutes to the pound plus 15 minutes over.

Nigel Gordon: Serve with a tasty wine gravy to make it more appetising.

Barbara Cartland: In Morocco the Moors believed implicitly that Honey was a love stimulant and large quantities of Honey were used in their marriage ceremonies, which often became sex orgies. The bride and bridegroom ate Honey and the wine and food were made with Honey.

Sweet and Sour Duck

from Gales Honey Bureau

Ingredients:

> 1 5lb. Duck
> 1 tblsp. Soya Sauce
> 10 ozs. Clear Honey
> 1 tblsp. Sweet Sherry

Method: Prick the duck all over with a carving fork and rub well with salt. Roast for ½ hour at 425°F, Mark 7.

Lower the heat to 375°F, Mark 5 and turn the duck over. Mix the honey, soya sauce and sherry together and spread some over the top of the duck. Continue roasting for 2½ hours turning the duck frequently and basting with the rest of the sauce.

Nigel Gordon: This results in a very flavourful duck with a delicious crispy crust. Serve garnished with watercress.

Barbara Cartland: In A.D. 23 Pliny the Elder who died during the eruption of Vesuvius, travelled in North Italy. He saw in the region of the River Po and the Appenines, 124 individuals who were all over a hundred, the eldest being 135. They were all bee-keepers!

MEAT DISHES

Honey-Glazed Baked Ham

from American Embassy Wives' Association

Ingredients:
>1 Ham
>¾ cup Pineapple Juice
>¾ cup Honey
>1 teasp. Mustard
>Pineapple Slivers
>Maraschino Cherries
>Cloves

Method: While ham is baking, mix pineapple juice, honey and mustard in a saucepan and simmer until mixture is thick. About 30 minutes before the ham is ready, spoon on the honey mixture and decorate with pineapple slices, cherries and cloves. Return to the oven for 30 minutes.

Nigel Gordon: If you do not want the sauce to be too thick dilute it with a little hot water.

Barbara Cartland: In Dalmatia the bridegroom's mother presented the bride with a spoonful of Honey and when the bride entered the house, everyone present sang:

30

"The bride comes in a happy hour,
    She has brought a blessing with her.
    Round her head there gleams the sunlight.
    In her hand there sits a falcon.
    Peace and concord brings she with her,
    In her mouth the honey's sweetness."

Heavenly Honeyed Ham

from Gales Honey Bureau

Ingredients:

    1 3 lb. Ham Joint
    6 ozs. Brown Sugar
    8 tblsps. Honey
    8 tblsps. Orange Juice
    ½ teasp. Colmans Mustard Powder

Method: Mix the sugar, mustard powder and 2 tblsps. Honey and spread half of this mixture over the ham. Place in a shallow roasting pan and bake at 325°F, Mark 3 for 1 hour. Heat the orange juice and the rest of the honey in a small pan and use this to baste the ham. Turn the oven up to 400°F, Mark 7, pour the remainder of the sugar and honey mixture over the joint and bake for a further 30 minutes when the ham will be a sticky golden-brown.

Nigel Gordon: This is a very succulent dish and a great success at a party.

Barbara Cartland: Ancient bee-keepers wanted bees to swarm so they would increase and bring them prosperity. But they believed the best result came from early swarming.

> "A swarm of bees in May
> Is worth a load of hay;
> A swarm of bees in June,
> Is worth a silver spoon;
> But a swarm in July,
> Is not worth a fly."

Honeyed Lamb

from Gales Honey Bureau

Ingredients:

> 2 Best Ends of Neck
> 3 Medium Onions
> 6 small Carrots
> 14 ozs. can Tomatoes
> 1 tblsp. Clear Honey
> 3 tblsps. Oil
> 1 teasp. Mustard Powder

Method: Heat the oil in a flameproof casserole and fry the sliced onion pieces until transparent. Rub the lamb with mustard powder, season with salt and pepper and brown in the oil. Add the chopped carrots to the pan and the tomatoes which have been strained from the juice. Put the juice into a measuring jug and stir in the honey, making the liquid up to half a pint with hot water. Pour over the meat and bring to the boil. Cover tightly and cook for 1½ hours at 375°F, Mark 5.

Nigel Gordon: Liquidize the sauce and serve separately.

Barbara Cartland: The Arabs are great admirers of strong sexual lovers. They eat a lot of lamb cooked in a delicious way and believe in the effect and power of Honey.

Sir Richard Burton translated a poem from *The Perfumed Garden*, a sixteenth century manual.

"The Negro Mimun, for full fifty days,
  Served numberless girls and gained honour and
    praise;
  And when he was asked to keep it up longer
  He did another ten days and finished up stronger!
  Now during this test, it was Honey and bread
  Enabled his *zabzab* to hold up its head."

Honeyed Lamb Chops

from New Zealand

Ingredients:

        4 Lamb Leg Chops
        1 oz. Butter
        1 teasp. Salt

¼ teasp. Pepper
¼ teasp. Ground Ginger
¼ cup Vinegar
2 tblsps. Honey
1 small Sweet Orange
1 small Lemon

Method: Trim the chops of the unnecessary fat. In a large pan heat the butter and brown the chops on both sides. Mix together the seasonings and vinegar and honey. Pour over the browned chops. Slice the orange and lemon finely discarding any pips and the end slices. Scatter the citrus rings over the top of the chops, cover with a close fitting lid and simmer for about 30 minutes or until the meat is tender. Serve the meat with the pan sauce and the citrus rings over the top of it and accompany with boiled rice.

Nigel Gordon: If you want the sauce sweeter, add some more honey and orange juice.

Barbara Cartland: Also in the *Perfumed Garden* is the following exhaltation:

"If a man will passionately give himself up to the enjoyment of coition without indulging too great fatigue, he must live upon strengthening foods—exciting comfits (these were mostly prepared with Honey), aromatic plants, meat, Honey, eggs, and similar viands."

34

Honeyed Pork Chops

from Gales Honey Bureau

Ingredients:

4 Loin Pork Chops
2 tblsps. Soy Sauce
1 tblsp. Clear Honey
1 clove Crushed Garlic

Method: Marinate the chops in a marinade made from the soy sauce, honey and garlic. Cover the dish and leave over night in the refrigerator or other cold place. When ready, drain them from the marinade and place in a casserole. Spoon the marinade over, cover and bake in the centre of the oven for 40 minutes at 375°F, Mark 5. Remove the lid and bake for a further 20 minutes. Serve with rice and decorate with parsley.

Nigel Gordon: Make sure that the pork is really done, as underdone pork is not very good for you.

Barbara Cartland: Honey has a soothing effect on the nerves and this is important for keeping people young. A spoonful of Honey when one is tense or tired enters the blood stream in 30 seconds. It gives a quick, effective "lift". There is no more effective tonic for "eternal energy"!

Loin of Pork

from Ted Moloney of Australia

Ingredients:

        1 2½ lb. Loin of Pork
        2 tblsps. Honey
        1 teasp. Cornflour
        1 Chicken Stock Cube
        1 dash Dry Sherry
        ¼ lb. Seedless White Grapes

Method: Put the honey over the pork and bake in the oven 375°F, Mark 5, basting frequently with honey until done. After removing from the oven pour off the fat for gravy and sprinkle the cornflour, add the stock cube, sherry and a little more honey to taste. When the grapes are in season add to the gravy.

Nigel Gordon: The crackling should take on a burnished brown glaze if it is frequently basted with honey. The meat soaks in some of the honey and gives a sweetness which suits it. Another thing is to rub a little oil on the crackling before going in the oven.

Barbara Cartland: Ted Moloney is Australia's most famous cook and food critic. He agrees with me that Honey is a magic substance which will strengthen our bodies, giving us energy and vitality, sharpening the brain, and is moreover a natural beautifier.

Roast Belly of Pork in Orange and Honey Sauce

from Gales Honey Bureau

Ingredients:

> 3 lbs. Joint Belly Pork
> 1 teasp. Salt
> 1 tblsp. Honey
> 1 tblsp. Undiluted Orange Juice
> 2 teasps. Gravy Powder
> ½ pint Water

Method: Score, roll and tie the joint into a neat shape. Sprinkle with the salt and roast in a moderate oven 350°F, Mark 4 for 35 minutes per pound and 35 minutes over. Remove joint onto a warm serving dish, skim surplus fat from the roasting tin, stir in the honey and orange. Moisten the gravy with a little of the water, add the rest of the water to the roasting tin and stir well. Bring the juices to the boil in a small saucepan, stir in the gravy mix and cook, stirring over a low heat until thick and smooth. If a crisp crackling is not required, brush the skin of the joint with a little extra clear honey 30 minutes before end of cooking time.

Nigel Gordon: Ask your butcher to chine the bone, or bone, roll and tie the joint for you to facilitate carving. Also you can use fresh orange juice but you must use the grated zest of 1 orange with it as well.

Barbara Cartland: When a male child is born in India

honey is used in the birth-rite and while certain special formulae are recited the father of the child feeds the baby with Honey, saying:

"I give thee honey food so that the gods may protect thee and that thou mayest live a hundred autumns in this world."

Roast Pork (*Chinese style*)

from Hong Kong (Recipe from Mrs. Lucy Lo)

Ingredients:

1½ lbs. Pork Fillet
2 tblsps. Honey
1 tblsp. Light Soya Sauce
1 tblsp. Soya Bean Paste
2 tblsps. Chinese Wine or
   Amontillado Sherry
½ teasp. Salt
1 Shallot (chopped fine)
1 Clove of Garlic
1 teasp. Sesame Oil

Method: Wash pork, rub it dry and cut into pieces 6 inches by 1½ inches. Rub seasoning, except sesame oil and honey, over pork and allow to marinate for one hour. Put skewers through pork and grill for about thirty minutes. Brush pork with honey and sesame oil and grill for another ten minutes. Garnish with tomato slices and serve.

Nigel Gordon: These ingredients can be bought from any Chinese or Health Shops. This makes a delightful dish for large parties.

Barbara Cartland: I had the most marvellous Chinese dinner I have ever eaten in Mrs. Lo's house in Hong Kong. The Chinese are centuries-old experts in food and medicine, both of which contain a lot of honey. The Chinese, I am convinced, knew about Royal Jelly and the miraculous Propolis long before the West, but only now are their ancient secrets being revealed to us.

Honeyed Beef Stew

from Gales Honey Bureau

Ingredients:

> 2 lbs. Stewing Beef
> 1 large Onion
> 2 tblsps. Honey
> Juice of 1 Lemon
> 2 teasps. Mustard Powder
> 1 Medium Green Pepper
> 6 ozs. Tomato Ketchup
> 3 stalks Celery
> ¾ pint Water

Method: Heat a little oil in a pan. Cut meat into cubes and brown in the hot fat. Slice the onion and pepper, chop the celery and add to the beef. Mix together the remaining ingredients and pour over the casserole. Cover and cook gently for 1½ hours at 350°F, Mark 4 or until meat is tender.

Nigel Gordon: Add a few chopped walnuts in this recipe to make it a very tasty dish.

Barbara Cartland: In 1950 the Russians issued a postage stamp in honour of Eicarov Mamoud Baguir-Ogly who had reached the age of 148. He was a bee-keeper!

Honey Garlic Spare-Ribs

from Canada

Ingredients:

3 lbs. Spare-ribs
½ cup Honey
¼ cup Lemon Juice
½ cup Water
3 tblsps. Tomato Ketchup
2 cloves Crushed Garlic
1 teasp. Salt
1 teasp. Ginger

Method: Season spare-ribs with salt and pepper, cover with foil and bake at 350°F, Mark 4 until almost tender. Combine remaining ingredients and pour over partly-cooked ribs. Marinate for several hours. Drain ribs and heat remaining sauce for basting. Place spare-ribs on greased rack about 5 inches from heat and broil until tender (about 20 minutes). Turn 3 or 4 times during cooking, basting with warm sauce.

Nigel Gordon: This is an inexpensive way of serving spare-ribs in the popular Canadian way.

Barbara Cartland: Both in Germany and Scotland, the belief existed that the souls of men departed their bodies in the form of bees. In Britain, as in Europe, it was customary to "tell" the bees whenever someone in the family died.

The widow went to the hive, rapped three times and said:

> "Bees, bees, thy master is dead,
>   Fly not away, but remain to comfort me."

PUDDINGS

Baklava

from Greece

Ingredients:

- 1 lb. Puff Pastry
- 1½ cups Butter
- 1 lb. Walnuts
- ½ cup Dry Breadcrumbs
- ¼ cup Sugar
- 1 teasp. Cinnamon
- ½ teasp. Cloves
- 4 cups Sugar (for the syrup)
- 2 cups Water
- Juice of 1 Lemon

Method: Roll out the pastry wafer thin and cut into large squares. Place the squares in a well buttered 9″ × 13″ baking pan and brush with butter. Repeat until 6 layers of buttered pastry sheets have been built up. Mix the walnuts breadcrumbs, sugar, cinnamon and cloves and sprinkle top pastry sheet with this mixture. Place two buttered pastry sheets over this. Repeat in the same manner until all the ingredients have been used ending with 6 pastry sheets.

Brush top with remaining butter and trim edges with a sharp knife. Cut into diagonal lines, the length of the pan to make diamond shaped pieces and sprinkle with water. Bake in a moderate oven 350°F, Mark 4 for 1 hour or until golden. Prepare the syrup, boil sugar, water and lemon juice for 10 minutes. Pour hot syrup over cooked Baklava. Allow to stand several hours before serving.

Nigel Gordon: The proper pastry to use in this recipe is called Phyllo and comes from Greece, but as it is difficult to obtain in this country, I sometimes use Puff Pastry thinly rolled out.

Barbara Cartland: Swami Sivananda the Yogi claims— "Honey will strengthen a weak heart, a weak brain and a weak stomach."

Champagne and Honey Sorbet

from Moet & Chandon (London) Ltd.

Ingredients:

> ¾ pint Cane Sugar Syrup
> 1 quart Bottle of Champagne
> Juice of 1 Lemon
> 1 stiffly beaten Egg White
> 2 ozs. Caster Sugar
> 1 dstsp. Honey

Method: Freeze the cane sugar syrup, champagne and lemon juice in a sorbetière. When it is half frozen, fold in the egg white, sugar and honey and put back into freezer to harden. Serve in frozen sorbet glasses.

Nigel Gordon: For this dish you can substitute the champagne, as it is a bit expensive, with a good sparkling wine, and the sugar cane with fruit sugar which is made from grapes.

Barbara Cartland: This is so delicious and so exciting it should be kept only for those in love. Madame de Pompadour believed that Champagne improved the skin. Cleopatra used Honey on her immortal face and bathed her lovely body in asses milk.

Flambee'd Apples in Honey

from Auberge de l'Illhäusern

Ingredients:
>   2 lbs. Cooking Apples
>   1 oz. Butter
>   1 tblsp. Honey
>   1 tblsp. Kirsch

Method: Sprinkle finely sliced cooking apples with lemon juice. In a flambée pan melt the butter and honey. As soon as the honey becomes lightly caramelized add the sliced apple. Allow to boil for a few moments until the apples are cooked. Sprinkle with the kirsch and set alight.

Nigel Gordon: This is delicious with vanilla ice-cream made with a real vanilla pod.

Barbara Cartland: The food in this three star restaurant is simply fabulous and I loved every mouthful. Swami Sivananda, from centuries of Yoga knowledge, says:

"Honey is a heart stimulant. It is useful in cases of malnutrition. It should be given for general physical repair. Honey kills bacteria and thus enables the body to overcome diseases. Disease germs cannot grow in Honey. Honey is substituted for orange juice and cod-liver oil. It is useful in bronchial catarrh, sore throat, coughs and colds.

"Honey can be taken with milk, cream or butter. It is a restorative after serious illness. It enters into the combination of Chavan Prash and other kalpas (ancient Hindu medicine). As soon as a child is born its tongue is smeared with Honey. This is the first food that the child takes.

"Honey is more stimulating than alcohol. If you take a tablespoonful of Honey in hot water when you are tired or exhausted by over-exertion, it will brace you up immediately. Soak ten almonds in water overnight. Remove the skins in the morning. Take them with two tablespoons of Honey. This is a brain tonic."

Honey Apple Crisp

from Canada

Ingredients:

>2 lbs. Cooking Apples
>1 tblsp. Lemon Juice
>½ cup Honey
>⅓ cup Plain Flour
>⅔ cup Rolled Oats
>½ cup Brown Sugar
>¼ teasp. Salt
>⅓ cup Butter

Method: Arrange apples in a greased baking dish and sprinkle with lemon juice. Spread honey over apples. Mix the flour, oats, sugar and salt and cut in butter until mixture resembles coarse breadcrumbs. Sprinkle over apples and bake at 375°F, Mark 5 until apples are tender and crust is browned.

Nigel Gordon: This dish is most delicious and like the traditional apple crumble only better.

Barbara Cartland: When Sir Edmund Hilary reached the top of Mount Everest, his father who was a New Zealand bee-keeper remarked: "It was all done on Honey". Tiger Tensing who accompanied him is a great honey-eater as are all the Sherpa porters. The best Honey I have ever eaten comes from the Himalayas and is carried 30 miles on the Sherpas' backs.

Honey Bananas

from South African Bee Journal

Ingredients:

> 4 Firm Bananas
> 2 tblsps. Oil
> $\frac{1}{3}$ cup Honey
> 1 teasp. Vinegar
> $\frac{1}{2}$ teasp. Cinnamon

Method: Cut the bananas cross-wise in halves or thirds. Brown lightly in the oil. Combine $\frac{3}{4}$ cup water, the honey and vinegar and simmer for 10 minutes or until thick. Pour over bananas, heat and sprinkle with the cinnamon.

Nigel Gordon: This is a sunny dish from a sunny climate.

Barbara Cartland: One of the most enthusiastic advocates of Honey is Bernard Mcfadden, Father of Modern Physical Culture. For more than half a century he has written and lectured about food and advised the use of Honey in place of other sweeteners.

Macfadden carried out hundreds of experiments with his own body, to find out what it could and could not do; to discover how little he could live on without falling ill; to discover what was the finest food for giving energy. At one time he walked bare-foot every morning from his home in the country to his office in the city, a distance of 23 miles. And all the sustenance he needed was a glass of water to which a spoon of Honey was added.

This remarkable man married again when well over 80, and made a parachute jump on every birthday, just to show that there was still a kick left in him.

Honey Coffee Mousse

from Canada

Ingredients:

> ½ teasp. Gelatine
> 2 tblsps. Cold Water
> ½ cup Strong Coffee
> ½ cup Honey
> 1 cup Cream (whipped)
> dash Nutmeg

Method: Soak gelatine in cold water for 5 minutes, dissolve in hot coffee and add honey. Chill, stirring occasionally until mixture has thickened, beat until foamy. Fold in whipped cream and turn in a soufflé dish. Freeze until firm.

Nigel Gordon: If you use instant coffee, dissolve 2 teasps. in half a cup of boiling water.

Barbara Cartland: Professor Dr. E. Koch, the famous German heart specialist, advocates Honey for the heart —He says:

"Honey is an ideal medicine, which one should take when there are to be increased exertions on the heart, for instance, bodily strains, before operations, etc. There is an old slogan: 'Honey is oats for the heart'."

Honey Syllabub

from Gales Honey Bureau

Ingredients:
> 1 pint Double Cream
> 6 tblsps. Clear Honey
> ¼ pint Dry Sherry or White Wine
> 2 tblsps. Lemon Juice

Method: Whisk all the ingredients until stiff enough to spoon into glasses. Almost fill the glasses then chill.

Nigel Gordon: Serve the Syllabub with ice-cream wafers or shortbread fingers and garnish each with orange or lemon slices.

Barbara Cartland: Dr. G. N. W. Thomas of Edinburgh writing in *The Lancet* said:

"In heart weaknesses, I have found honey to have a marked effect in reviving the heart action and keeping patients alive. I have further evidence of this in a recent case of pneumonia. The patient consumed two pounds of honey during the illness; there was a marked early crisis with no subsequent rise in temperature and an exceptionally good pulse. I suggest honey should be given for general physical repair and above all, for heart failure."

Loukmades

from Greece

Ingredients:

$\frac{1}{2}$ oz. Beer Yeast
3 ozs. Self-Raising Flour
1 pinch Salt
3 tblsps. Honey
2 tblsps. Hot Water
1 tblsp. Crushed Almonds
1 tblsp. Brown Sugar
1 pinch Cinnamon

Method: Mix the yeast, flour and salt with enough warm water to make a thick consistency (thin enough to pour) and let it stand for an hour to rise. Heat up some oil in a deep pan, grasp a handful of the dough with your left hand, and with your right, detach little dollops which you throw into the boiling oil.

Next to you, you have a bowl of honey and hot water mixed and into that you throw the piping hot Loukmades. Remove to a hot dish. Mix the almonds, sugar and cinnamon and sprinkle on the Loukmades. They are ready to serve.

Nigel Gordon: The Loukmades should be like little golden balls full of nothing except hot air. Additional thick honey should be ready on the table for those who have a particularly sweet tooth. The best honey is Hymethis, the Greek honey.

Barbara Cartland: Jim Londos, world heavyweight wrestler in the nineteen thirties, was a Greek. He was about five feet eight inches tall and beautifully proportioned. His diet was as ancient as Greece itself— Honey.

The greatest of all Indian wrestlers, Gama the Tiger, the man who put the giant Pole, Vladivas Zbyscko on his back in a matter of seconds, ate a great deal of honey in milk and sweets every day. The sweets favoured by all Indian wrestlers and strong men—*labri, ludoos* and *saundaesh* are all made with honey.

Mock Vatalappan

(Honey pudding)
from Sri Lanka

Ingredients:

$\frac{1}{4}$ oz. China-moss
5 ozs. Brown Sugar
1$\frac{1}{2}$ cups Milk
1 Egg Yolk
1 well-beaten Egg White
1 pinch of Salt

53

Grated Nutmeg
A few Chopped Roasted
Cashewnuts

Method: Chop the China-moss into small pieces, add it to a large bowl and let it soak for three hours in 4 cups of water. Drain the China-moss, and discard the water. Put the sugar and milk into a saucepan and heat over a low heat, add the china-moss and cook until moss is dissolved. Remove from the heat, let it stand for a few minutes, then add the beaten egg yolk and honey. Gently fold in the beaten egg white, salt and nutmeg. Pour into a glass dish and let it set well. Sprinkle well with the cashewnuts.

Nigel Gordon: The China-moss is a form of gelatine and can be bought from any Indian or Chinese food shop. If you have difficulty in getting this, use ½ oz. of gelatine to ¼ pint of water and follow the recipe. Serve with whipped cream.

Barbara Cartland: Honey products are at last being recognized as the greatest benefit inside and outside our bodies. Besides the new and fabulous Propolis, the greatest antibiotic the world has ever known, which cures ulcers and colitis, acne and sore-throats, there is Florapoll from Vienna for vitality and Melbrosia which rejuvenates both men and women.

Normandy Apple Tart

from Gales Honey Bureau

Ingredients:

        2 lbs. Cooking Apples
        5 tblsps. Honey
        2 small Lemons
        1 oz. Butter
        1 teasp. Cinnamon
        6 ozs. Shortcrust Pastry
        3 Eating Apples

Method: Peel and core the cooking apples, slice and cook gently with 3 tblsps. water in a covered pan until soft. Add 3 tblsps. honey, grated rind of one of the lemons, butter and cinnamon and simmer uncovered until reduced to a thick purée. Allow to cool. Roll out the pastry and line an 8 inch flan ring. Pour on the apple purée. Core the eating apples but do not peel, halve them and slice very thinly. Arrange on top of the purée and bake for 30 minutes at 400°F, Mark 7.

Place the remaining honey in a pan with the juice of half a lemon and heat gently until honey dissolves and brush over the tart to give a shiny glaze.

Nigel Gordon: If you happen to have any spare brandy or cooking sherry then add 1 tblsp. to the purée to give it that extra taste.

Barbara Cartland: Honey should always be given to children in the water they drink from their fruit bottle.

It is not only far, far better for babies than sugar, it also gives them the minerals they need for their strong bodies.

These include copper, iron, silicon, manganese, calcium, chlorine, sodium, potassium, sulphur, phosphorus, and magnesium.

Poires Au Cognac

from Gales Honey Bureau

Ingredients:

       6 Conference Pears
       3 tblsps. Caster Sugar
       3 tblsps. Water
       6 tblsps. Honey
       2 tblsps. Brandy

Method: Peel the pears but leave them whole. Put the sugar and water in a pan and gently heat the mixture, stirring frequently, until the sugar has dissolved. Stir in the honey, add the pears and poach them over a low heat until they are tender. Do not let them go mushy, they must retain their shape. Let the pears cool in the syrup, basting occasionally. Stir in the brandy and chill.

Serve the pears in a shallow dish with the syrup poured around. Whipped cream can be served with them.

Nigel Gordon: You can use peaches for this recipe,

provided you keep them whole. They are equally as nice as the pears.

Barbara Cartland: Honey has been used lately in the prevention of bed-wetting. Children who wet the bed at night are nearly always nervous. Honey has a double effect. First, it acts as a sedative to the child's nervous system. Second, it will attract and hold fluid, sparing the kidneys and strengthening the bladder, with the result that the child does not wet the bed during the night. Give your child one teaspoonful of Honey at bedtime.

Strawberry Fool

from Gales Honey Bureau

Ingredients:

      1 lb. Strawberries
      ½ pint Double Cream
      1 tblsp. Honey
      1 teasp. Chopped Almonds

Method: Rub ¾ lb. of strawberries through a fine sieve and slice the rest. Pour the cream and honey into a bowl and whisk until thick. Fold in the strawberry purée and the slices. Serve in small individual glasses or dishes and decorate with almonds.

Nigel Gordon: As I said before, put the strawberries in

the liquidizer before sieving. This dish can be done with raspberries or blackcurrants.

Barbara Cartland: Wives who want their husbands to make love to them have lots of Honey on the menu. This is well known in Hawaii where the romantic islands abound with stories of the effectiveness of their special Kiawe Blossom Honey. Personally in the years I've advocated Honey I find all Honey helps both men and women to feel warm and loving.

Honeyed Rice Bake

Ingredients:

> 1 Lemon
> 1 cup Rice
> 2¾ cups Milk
> ¾ cup Honey
> ½ cup Sultanas
> 2 ozs. Chopped Walnuts
> 1 oz. Butter
> ½ teasp. Cinnamon
> 2 Eggs
> ½ cup Castor Sugar

Method: Peel some strips of rind from the lemon and put them with the juice of the lemon, the rice and milk into a saucepan and cook slowly for 15 minutes, stirring occasionally. Heat the honey and add it to the sultanas, walnuts, butter and cinnamon. Remove the lemon strips from the rice and stir in the honey mixture and the egg yolks. Put the mixture into a greased pie-dish. Beat the egg whites until stiff, gradually adding the sugar. Arrange on the rice and bake in a moderate oven 350°F, Mark 4, for 20 minutes.

Nigel Gordon: Serve with stewed or fresh fruit.

Barbara Cartland: Honey is marvellous for older people because it reduces anaemia. Honey helps to maintain the right balance in one's blood and this of course is tremendously important as one gets older. Dr. Arnold Lorand who wrote a book called *Old Age Deferred* says:

"As the best food for the heart I recommend Honey. Honey is easily digested and assimilated, and it's the best sweet food as it does not cause flatulence and can prevent it to a certain extent, promoting the activity of the bowels."

Pancakes with Honey Soufflé Filling

from Moet & Chandon (London) Ltd.

Ingredients:
       ½ pint Crême Patissière
       3 teasps. Honey
       1 dstsp. Raisins soaked in Champagne
       4 Stiffly-beaten Egg Whites
       4 Pancakes
       4 ozs. Brown Sugar
       ½ cup Water

Method: Make ½ pint of the crême patissière. While hot, add the honey and raisins. Fold in the beaten egg whites. Spread the mixture over the pancakes and roll them. Place in a baking dish and cook in a hot oven 400°F, Mark 7 for 10 minutes. In a small saucepan, place the sugar and water and bring to the boil until thick. Pour caramel mixture on waxed paper and allow to harden. Crush and sprinkle caramelized sugar over pancakes before serving.

Nigel Gordon: If you don't want to use Champagne to soak the raisins use a very good white wine.

Barbara Cartland: It seems a mundane thought when this dish is so delicious but Dr. Olaf Martensen-Larsen who is the leading expert on alcoholism in Denmark, discovered that Honey is the most effective cure for a 'hangover'. Dr. Larson advises the patient to eat a quarter of a pound of pure Honey, wait half-an-hour, then eat another quarter of a pound.

Nusspotitze

from Austria

Ingredients:

5 ozs. Butter
2½ ozs. Sugar
3 Egg Yolks
1 oz. Yeast
¼ pint Milk

10 ozs. Flour
1 teasp. Grated Lemon Rind

Filling:

1 lb. Walnuts
6 ozs. Sugar
¼ pint Rum
⅜ pint Honey
2 tblsps. Raisins
1 teasp. Grated Lemon Rind
1 teasp. Lemon Juice
Pinch Cinnamon
⅛ pint Cream

Method: Butter and flour a savarin tin. Cream yeast with a little of the sugar, add tepid milk. Add a pinch of flour and put in a warm place to set. Cream the butter and sugar and add egg yolks. Add the flour alternately with yeast and milk. Beat well with a wooden spoon until dough comes away clean from the spoon. Sprinkle pastry board with flour and spread dough over, cover with the filling, roll up and set in the savarin tin. Put in a warm place, cover with a cloth and leave to rise for 40 minutes, then bake in the oven for 1 hour at 375°F, Mark 5.

For the filling put all the ingredients except honey and rum in a bowl. Heat the honey and stir into other ingredients and then add the rum.

Nigel Gordon: This is a good recipe for someone with a large family as it is very filling and goes a long way.

Barbara Cartland: In Ancient Egypt Honey was used for embalming and it is still used in Burma. Honey is a preservative in cakes and sweetmeats and is always used in an Indian household. Honey preserves all food in a climate where everything decomposes rapidly.

VEGETABLES AND STARTERS

Carrots Vichy

from Ted Moloney from Australia

Ingredients:

> 1 lb. Young Small Carrots
> 4 ozs. Butter
> 1 tblsp. Honey
> Salt and Pepper
> Parsley for Garnish

Method: Melt the butter in a heavy saucepan. As the butter bubbles add carrots and sprinkle with salt and pepper. Cover and simmer over a low heat for 20 minutes or until tender. Remove the lid and raise the heat. Stir in the honey and some parsley and continue stirring until carrots are glazed and slightly browned. Serve and sprinkle parsley over them.

Nigel Gordon: This can be done with older carrots, but they have to be boiled for 5 minutes and then sliced less than $\frac{1}{4}$ inch thick.

Barbara Cartland: Honey at night makes one sleep. My Mother who is 98 takes Honey every night in hot water or hot milk when she goes to bed. I am also convinced that the reason she is active and has all her faculties is

64

because she has eaten honey all through her long life. And perhaps her sympathy, her understanding, the warmth and the love she gives her children, grandchildren and great-grandchildren also owe something to the Magic of Honey.

Californian Lunch Salad with Honey Dressing

from Gales Honey Bureau

Ingredients:

> 1 Large Melon
> 8 ozs. Cottage Cheese
> 2 ozs. Mixed Chopped Nuts
> 2 Oranges
> 2 Grapefruit
> Chives
> Juice of 2 small Oranges
> 1 teasp. Grated Orange Rind
> 1 tblsp. Clear Honey
> 1 squeeze Lemon Juice
> Mint

Method: Peel the oranges and grapefruit and separate into segments. Mix together with the cheese and nuts. Cut the melon into a basket and remove the flesh either with a melon ball or scoop or by cutting carefully. Dice if necessary and add to the salad mixture. Just before serving toss the salad in the honey dressing and pile into the basket. For the dressing, you mix all the ingredients together, chill and then shake well, before using.

Nigel Gordon: The Melon looks far more decorative if the flesh is scooped with a melon ball scoop and also you can give it an extra colour by decorating with cocktail cherries.

Barbara Cartland: Honeys in America range from water white of which an example is Willowherb or Fireweed because it grows where fires have been, to Tupelo blossom Honey from Florida. Blueberry blossom Honey contains large amounts of iron and is especially recommended to anaemic persons while Onion blossom Honey has no flavour of the onion since Honey is made from the blossoms and not from the fruit of the plant. Nevertheless it has all the therapeutic value of "Granny's old fashioned Onion Tea" for treating colds, bronchitis and other respiratory ailments.

Glazed Mixed Vegetables

from Gales Honey Bureau

Ingredients:
> 1 lb. Small Onions (peeled)
> 1 lb. Carrots (peeled and diced)
> 1 lb. Turnips (peeled and diced)
> 1 oz. Butter
> 1 tblsp. Clear Honey

Method: Cook onions in boiling salted water for 10 minutes, add carrots and turnips and cook for a further 10 minutes. Drain. Melt butter and honey in a saucepan, add vegetables and cook, stirring occasionally, over a moderate heat, until vegetables are well glazed. Serve hot.

Nigel Gordon: This is a very economical dish and filling.

Barbara Cartland: Honey is a marvellous preventative of bronchitis. This terrible ailment results every year in far greater loss of manpower than strikes or any disease. My husband was shot by a sniper at the battle of Passchendaele and lost one lung. After I married him I was told it was unlikely he would live long and he suffered every year from really terribly bad bronchitis. I gave him a teaspoonful of comb Honey every night and morning. He lived until he was sixty-five and very seldom had any trouble with bronchitis.

Glazed Onions

from Gales Honey Bureau

Ingredients:
> 1 lb. Medium-sized Onions (peeled)
> 1 oz. Butter
> 1 tblsp. Clear Honey
> Pinch Ground Cloves

Method: Cook onions in boiling salted water for about 15 minutes, until just tender, then drain. Melt butter and honey in a saucepan, add ground cloves and onions, and cook over a moderate heat, stirring occasionally, until the glaze thickens, and begins to coat the onions.

Nigel Gordon: This is very nice with braised beef.

Barbara Cartland: In 400 B.C. the great doctor Hypocrates recommended Honey as a means of curing ulcers. There was an old woman in my village who had very bad ulcers on her legs, I suggested to the District Nurse who had tried every sort of remedy that she should use honey under the bandages. I also gave the old woman some multi-vitamin tablets and several pots of Honey. In three months her legs were practically healed.

Honey Baked Potatoes

from Gales Honey Bureau

Ingredients:

> 2 lbs. Potatoes (peeled)
> Salt
> 2 ozs. Butter
> 2 tblsps. Clear Honey
> 1 oz. Chopped Walnuts

Method: Halve or quarter large potatoes and put into a pan of cold salted water, bring to the boil and simmer for 15 minutes. Drain. Turn potatoes into a roasting tin and dot with butter. Spoon honey over potatoes, then sprinkle walnuts on top. Roast in a hot oven 425°F, Mark 7 for about 1 hour turning the potatoes occasionally. Sprinkle salt over potatoes before serving.

Nigel Gordon: You can do this recipe with potatoes in their jackets. Do not boil them.

Barbara Cartland: Bees sometimes fly as far as two miles for nectar. It needs 10,000 flights for a bee to convey a pound of nectar to the hive. Their productivity is immense. The Queen can lay 3,000 eggs only, upon the workers activity depends much of the fertility of our seeds. Can you be surprised that Honey gives us strength and energy?

Sweet and Sour Cabbage

from Gales Honey Bureau

Ingredients:

> 1 White Cabbage
> 2 ozs. Butter
> 2 tblsps. Clear Honey
> 2 tblsps. Lemon Juice
> $\frac{1}{4}$ teasp. Caraway Seeds

Method: Prepare and shred cabbage. Cook in a little boiling salted water for 5 minutes, then drain. Melt butter and honey in a saucepan, add lemon juice, cabbage and caraway seeds. Cook gently for about 10 minutes, until cabbage is tender, stirring occasionally.

Nigel Gordon: This cabbage can be used cold for salads.

Barbara Cartland: Yehudi Menuhin the world famous violinist practises Yoga every day and takes warm milk and Honey before every performance and rosehip tea and Honey during the interval. Those who work with him say he is never ill and never temperamental.

Avocado in Honey

from Moet & Chandon (London) Ltd.

Ingredients:
>   1 Avocado Pear
>   1 tblsp. Thin Honey
>   1 tblsp. Flaked Toasted Almonds
>   1 tblsp. Brown Sugar
>   1 tblsp. Water

Method: Split the avocado down the middle lengthwise and remove the skin intact making two half shells. Cut the avocado pear into $\frac{1}{2}$ inch cubes in a mixing bowl and gently coat with honey. Replace the avocado mixture in the skin shells and scatter with toasted almonds.

In a small saucepan place sugar and water and bring to the boil until thick. Pour caramel mixture on waxed paper and allow to harden. Crush and sprinkle caramel-ized sugar on top of the avocado.

Nigel Gordon: As a substitute for almonds take a dried avocado stone and peel the skin off. Roast in the oven and crush with a hammer. Also if the honey is too thick, place in a mixing bowl placed in hot water until desired consistency is obtained.

Barbara Cartland: The United States Bureau of Ento-mology in Washington have found that placed in Honey the germ that causes dysentery dies within 48 hours, that the chronic bronco-pneumonia germs die on the fourth day, and the germ that causes typhoid—and may cause peritonitis—on the fifth day. All these die in far quicker time than could be achieved by penicillin or any other antibiotic.

SOUPS AND SAVOURIES

Cold Raspberry Soup

from Gales Honey Bureau

Ingredients:

1 lb. Fresh Raspberries
1 small carton Sour Cream
2 tblsps. Honey
5 tblsps. Red Wine

Method: Rub raspberries through a fine sieve. Put the honey together with 2 tblsps. of the red wine and 2 tblsps. water in a small saucepan and heat gently until the honey has dissolved. Leave for a few minutes to cool and then stir into the raspberry purée. Stir in half the cream. Add the rest of the wine and one third of a pint of cold water. Stir and chill for several hours.

Nigel Gordon: Put the raspberries in a liquidizer and then through a fine sieve. You will find this is much the easiest way to do it. Serve the soup with small blobs of sour cream floating on the top.

Barbara Cartland: One of the best Honeys for cooking is Australian Light Amber. It is also one of the cheapest. Gathered from the blossoms of the Gum Tree and Mimosa Flowers it is used as the basis of cough syrup because of its beneficial demulcent properties.

Savoury Pancake Dish

from Gales Honey Bureau

Ingredients:

$\frac{1}{2}$ lb. Lean Bacon
6 Pancakes
2 tblsps. Honey
1 teasp. Cinnamon

Method: Cut the slices of bacon into small pieces and sauté until crisp. Make pancakes and place the bacon in the middle. Roll up and place in the oven 300°F, Mark 1 for 15 minutes. Sprinkle with the honey and cinnamon and serve hot.

Nigel Gordon: You can make this dish like an omelette then sprinkle with the honey and cinnamon when it is ready.

Barbara Cartland: I often think of a story about a man who had a petrol filling station in the Arizona desert. It was miles from anywhere, but he and his wife made a living from the trucks and the occasional travellers who passed by. One day something went wrong and the gasoline tank blew up. In trying to put the fires out the owner was most terribly burnt. There was no medicament in the house which they could use to alleviate the terrible pain. Fortunately they had only that very day taken the Honey from their hives, so the wife and the mother of the burnt man covered him in Honey, and wrapping him with gauze like a cocoon, they put him in a car and rattled him 15 miles over dusty, bumpy roads to the nearest hospital.

From the moment the Honey was applied the victim suffered no pain, what is more the burns healed without leaving a scar.

Honey Cheese Pie

from Canada

Ingredients:

½ lb. Shortcrust Pastry
8 ozs. Cream Cheese
3 Eggs
½ cup Liquid Honey
½ cup Light Cream
½ cup Milk
¼ teasp. Salt
1 teasp. Grated Lemon Rind
1 tblsp. Lemon Juice

Method: Bake pie shell for 10 minutes at 425°F, Mark 7. Cream the cheese. Beat eggs, add honey, cream, milk, salt and lemon rind. Add egg mixture gradually to the cheese and beat until smooth, add lemon juice. Pour mixture into partly baked pie shell and bake at 350°F, Mark 4 until filling is firm. Chill and decorate top with glazed fruit such as blueberries, cherries, or peaches.

Nigel Gordon: This pie is delicious and much lighter if you use puff pastry.

Barbara Cartland: Everyone knows the magnificent and delectable Clover Honey from Canada. Buck wheat is also part of this country's Honey crop. Dark amber in colour it is full of mineral goodness and essentially good for chest complaints. Alfalfa sweet clover and alsike clover produce valuable forage crops for animals and delicious Honey. The roots go down as far as 30 feet and I recommend tablets with Alfalfa for those who are physically and mentally depleted by long illnesses.

CAKES AND GATEAUX

Freiburger Leckerli

from Brenner's Park Hotel, Baden-Baden

Ingredients:

        1 lb. Honey
        10 ozs. Sugar
        1½ lbs. Flour
        3½ ozs. Candied Lemon Peel
        3½ ozs. Candied Orange Peel
        3½ ozs. Chopped Almonds
        2 tblsps. Kirsh
        1 teasp. Cinnamon
        ½ oz. Clove
        5 drops Lemon Concentrate
        1 teasp. Ground Anise
        1 teasp. Nutmeg
        1 teasp. Gardamon
        pinch Hartshorn Salt
        1 teasp. Baking Powder

Method: Heat mixture of honey and sugar until dissolved, and allow to cool to luke-warm state. Then mix flour, almonds, hazelnuts, lemon and orange peel, and spice. Add mixture of honey and sugar, then knead to a smooth dough. When dough has cooled fully, add kirsch, salt and baking powder and again mix thoroughly.

80

Roll dough to fit the baking plate and bake at moderate heat 350°F, Mark 4, for 30 minutes. While still hot glaze with sugar and egg whites. Beat egg whites to a stiff snow. Boil sugar to a thread and stir into egg snow while still hot. When cooled cut the Leckerli into square pieces.

Nigel Gordon: The Gardamon is a raising component, and the Hartshorn salt is Carbonate of Ammonia.

Barbara Cartland: I was given this in the beautiful hotel which is part of the history of Baden-Baden. It is here the famous French Courtesans stayed in the years of the Second Empire when Baden was a summer Capital of Europe,—spoken of as the Pearl of the Black Forest. They stayed in the town with its French influence, gambled away fortunes in the Casino and ate the succulent Black Forest Honey which has a flavour all of its own.

Black Forest Honey Cake

from Brenner's Park Hotel, Baden-Baden

Ingredients:

> 9¼ ozs. Honey
> 4 ozs. Sugar
> ¾ oz. Butter
> 2½ ozs. Chopped Almonds
> 1½ ozs. Lemon Peel

2 tblsps. Kirsh
1 pinch Ground Clove
1 teasp. Cinnamon
4¾ fl. ozs. Milk
1 Egg
3 ozs. Cornflour
1 teasp. Baking Powder
9¼ ozs. Plain Flour

Method: Heat honey, sugar and butter to boiling point, then add milk, kirsh, almonds, lemon peel and egg. When mixture is luke-warm add the remaining ingredients, stir well, fill into greased box-type baking container. Bake at a moderate heat 350°F, Mark 4 for 1¼ hours.

Nigel Gordon: We found this cake a little bit dry so to moisten it a bit add more butter and kirsh.

Barbara Cartland: Hay-fever is very unpleasant and can make the sufferer miserable. Honeycomb is recommended for hay fever in *Folk Medicine* that wonderful book by Dr. D. C. Jarvis. If the patient will chew a teaspoonful of honeycomb whenever he has an attack, the hay fever usually vanishes within a few seconds. But note, it must be honeycomb.

Filled Honeycakes

from Austria

Ingredients:

¼ lb. Honey
2 ozs. Sugar
1 dstsp. Cinnamon
Pinch Cloves
½ lb. Plain Flour
½ teasp. Baking Powder
1 Egg
Halved Blanched Almonds

Filling:

2 ozs. Ground Hazel Nuts
2 ozs. Sugar
1 oz. Mixed Peel (chopped)
1 Egg

Method: Heat honey, then add cinnamon, cloves and sugar. Stir well and leave to cool. Add flour, previously sifted with the baking powder, and the egg. Knead well, cover with a cloth and leave overnight. Mix together the hazelnuts, sugar, mixed peel, and the egg for the filling. Roll out the dough to about one-eighth inch thickness, cut into shapes and spread half of them with the filling.

Place remaining honeycakes over the ones spread with filling, brush with egg white and decorate with halved blanched almonds, Bake at 325°F, Mark 3, for ½ hour.

Nigel Gordon: A delightful mixture of spices and honey straight from the Austrian Tyrol. This dish can be made with soft brown sugar.

Barbara Cartland: If you burn your finger while cooking cover with Honey (a thick one is best) and the pain will stop immediately. Bandage over a piece of lint or gauze and leave bandaged for at least four hours. It will heal without a scar.

Spiced Honey Cake

from Gales Honey Bureau

Ingredients:

2 ozs. Butter
5 ozs. Honey
5 ozs. Brown Sugar
10 ozs. Plain Flour
Pinch of Salt
1 teasp. Bicarbonate of Soda
1 teasp. Baking Powder
1 teasp. Mixed Spice
1 teasp. Cinnamon
1 teasp. Ground Ginger
3 ozs. Chopped Peel
1 Egg
¼ pint Milk
Flaked Almonds

84

Method: Melt the butter in a pan, draw off the heat and stir in honey and sugar. Cool. Sift the flour, salt, soda, baking powder, spice, cinnamon and ginger in a bowl. Add the peel. Beat up egg and milk and mix thoroughly with the cooled honey mixture. Pour into the flour and beat until smooth. Pour into a greased 1 lb. loaf tin lined at the bottom with greased paper. Scatter flaked almonds over and bake at 350°F, Mark 4 until firm (about 1¼ hours).

Nigel Gordon: Serve this cake with butter in the morning with coffee or as a spicy tea bread.

Barbara Cartland: Coffee Bloom Honey which comes from Costa Rica where the purest coffee in the world is grown, has the highest mineral content. Jamaican Logwood Honey is renowned for its astringent properties. The trace elements found in it include larger amounts of the B Complex vitamin than in other honeys.

Honeyed Ginger Bread

Ingredients:

       2 ozs. Butter
       5 ozs. Brown Sugar
       2 Eggs
       1 teasp. Grated Lemon Rind
       7 ozs. Plain Flour
       1 teasp. Nutmeg
       2 teasps. Baking Powder

1 Pinch Salt
2 teasps. Ginger
½ cup Honey
½ cup Black Treacle
¼ cup Boiling Water

Nigel Gordon: Cream the butter and sugar, then beat in the eggs and lemon rind. Sift the flour with the nutmeg, baking powder, salt and ginger. In a bowl mix the honey, treacle and water until well blended. Add the flour mixture alternately with the liquid to the butter and sugar mixture beating each time until well blended. Bake in a buttered square tin 8″×11″ in a moderate oven 350°F, Mark 4, for 60 minutes.

Barbara Cartland: The *Swiss Bee Journal* reported an experience with three groups of children, all in poor health. The first group was given a normal diet. The second was given a normal diet plus medication. The third the same diet plus Honey. The Honey-fed group of sick children "out distanced the other two in every respect—blood count, weight, energy, vivacity and general appearance."

Honey Date Loaf

from The Greek Embassy

Ingredients:

2 tblsps. Butter
½ cup Honey

1 Egg
1 teasp. Grated Lemon Rind
2 teasps. Lemon Juice
1½ cups Plain Flour
¼ teasp. Salt
⅛ teasp. Baking Soda
1 teasp. Baking Powder
½ cup Buttermilk
1 cup Chopped Dates
½ cup Chopped Walnuts

Method: Cream the butter and then beat in the honey, egg, lemon rind and juice. Combine flour, salt, baking soda and powder and add alternately with the buttermilk to the butter. Fold in the dates and walnuts. Turn into an oiled 9″×5″×3″ loaf tin and bake for 60 minutes in a preheated oven 350°F, Mark 4.

Nigel Gordon: Leave the loaf to get really cold then serve with lots of butter. If you want to put ginger in it, then add a teasp. to the flour mixture.

Barbara Cartland: Honey is one of the few great products that possess natural laxative properties. It is also one of the quickest stimulants known. One tablespoon in a cup of hot water in cases of shock, fainting or after haemorrhage is an instant restorative.

Honey Cookies

from The Greek Embassy

Ingredients:

$\frac{1}{3}$ cup Melted Butter
1 cup Honey (Hymethus)
2 Eggs
$\frac{1}{2}$ cup Milk
$3\frac{1}{2}$ cups Plain Flour
2 teasps. Baking Powder
$\frac{1}{2}$ teasp. Baking Soda
$\frac{1}{4}$ teasp. Salt
1 teasp. Cinnamon
$\frac{1}{2}$ teasp. Allspice
1 cup Chopped Mixed Dried Fruits
$\frac{1}{2}$ cup Sunflower Seed Kernels

Method: Combine butter and honey and stir in eggs and milk. Sift together flour, baking powder, soda, salt, cinnamon and allspice. Add fruits and kernels to flour mixture and stir into the honey mixture. Place by teaspoonfuls on an oiled or buttered baking sheet. Bake for 15 minutes in a pre-heated oven 375°F, Mark 5.

Nigel Gordon: For recipes with baking soda, use cornflour, if you find it difficult to get the soda.

Barbara Cartland: Greek Honey like Hymethus comes from a flower which grows on Mount Olympus, and has been known since ancient times as the Honey of the Gods. It is alleged to have a stimulating influence on the Sex glands. Honey is also aphrodisiac and for a loving, passionate husband use Hymethus in the cooking.

Honey Upside Down Cake

from American Embassy Wives' Association

Ingredients:

$1\frac{1}{2}$ cups Plain Flour
1 teasp. Baking Powder
$\frac{1}{4}$ teasp. Cornflour
$\frac{1}{4}$ teasp. Cinnamon
$\frac{1}{2}$ teasp. Nutmeg
Dash Ginger
$\frac{1}{2}$ cup Soft Butter
$\frac{3}{4}$ cup Honey
1 Egg
$\frac{1}{2}$ cup Milk

Topping
$\frac{1}{2}$ cup Honey
$\frac{1}{4}$ cup Butter
4 Cooking Apples
Maraschino Cherries

Sauce
$\frac{1}{2}$ cup Honey
$\frac{1}{2}$ cup Butter

Method: For the topping, put honey and butter in a heavy 10″ skillet and cook over a low heat until butter has melted. Core unpared apples and slice about $\frac{1}{2}″$ thick. Arrange enough of these slivers in the honey mixture to fit comfortably. Simmer gently, turning once, until apples are partly cooked. Put in a cherry in the centre of each apple ring and set aside.

For the cake batter, you sift the flour with the baking powder, cornflour, cinnamon, nutmeg and ginger. Beat butter and honey, add the egg and beat thoroughly. Stir in the flour mixture and milk and pour over the apple rings. Bake for 45 minutes in the oven 350°F, Mark 4 or until set. Turn upside down on a large platter and serve hot or cold with the sauce on the side. For the sauce, combine the honey with the butter and heat until butter has melted. Do not boil.

Nigel Gordon: Although this looks complicated, it is very easy and well worth it in the end, as it is a delicious cake and can be served either as a sweet or in the afternoon as a cake.

Barbara Cartland: Bees have no resistance to insecticides so however polluted the land may be with sprays and chemicals from where they gather the nectar they never carry the poisons back to the hive. They die first. This guarantees that all Honey is practically free from insecticide residues.

90

Sunny Honey Fudge

from New Zealand

Ingredients:
>2 ozs. Butter
>¼ cup Water
>2 tblsps. Clear Honey
>½ cup Sweetened Condensed Milk
>2 cups Sugar

Method: Put all the ingredients together in a heavy based saucepan, heat and stir gently until the sugar is dissolved. Bring to the boil and boil steadily on a moderate heat until a little of the mixture dropped into cold water will form a soft ball. This will take 12 minutes. Remove from the heat and beat with a wooden spoon until the mixture begins to thicken. Pour into a lightly greased 7″ tin and when cold but not firm, cut into small squares.

Nigel Gordon: This sweet is most delicious and one could not eat a lot unless they had a sweet tooth.

Barbara Cartland: The Maori in New Zealand uses the New Zealand Clover Honey, which is one of my favourites, for chest complaints. I find that taken at night, if one has a cold coming, as a hot drink following a glass containing 2 large teaspoonsful of Vit c, it is a really effective cold-killer! Athletes swear by it as a source of energy.

Honey Orange Bread

from New Zealand

Ingredients:

> 1 oz. Butter
> 1 cup Honey
> 1 Egg
> 1 teasp. Grated Orange Rind
> 2¾ cups Plain Flour
> 2½ teasps. Baking Powder
> ½ teasp. Cornflour
> ¾ cup Orange Juice
> ¼ cup Chopped Mixed Peel

Method: Melt the butter and blend with the honey, beat the egg and mix into the honey, add the grated rind. Sift the flour, baking powder and cornflour together and fold into the other mixture alternately with the orange juice, then stir in the peel.

Put the batter into a 10″ loaf tin which has been well greased and lined on the bottom with a piece of greaseproof paper. Bake at 350°F, Mark 4 for about 50 minutes.

Nigel Gordon: This loaf is much nicer if it is kept until the next day before cutting.

Barbara Cartland: New Zealand has delicious pure Honey from its great unspoilt stretches of open land. Those who poo-poo the properties of Honey never mention Dr. Schuette of the University of Wisconsin who has said that "dark Honey contains practically all the minerals comprising the human skeleton". Dark Honeys are produced in the late summer and generally have a stronger taste and a higher mineral content. I always give small children pale spring honeys like the New Zealand Clover Honey.

SAUCES

Honey Cinnamon Butter

Ingredients:

$\frac{1}{4}$ cup Butter
$\frac{1}{4}$ cup Honey
$\frac{1}{2}$ teasp. Cinnamon

Method: Cream the butter, honey and cinnamon. Spread on hot toast.

Honey Butter Sauce

Ingredients:

$\frac{3}{4}$ cup Honey
3 tblsps. Butter
1 teasp. Lemon Juice
$\frac{1}{4}$ teasp. Vanilla

Method: Heat the honey and butter until blended. Cool and add the lemon juice and vanilla. Serve with pancakes.

Honey Sauce

Ingredients:

¼ cup Honey
2 tblsps. Lemon Juice
2 tblsps. Butter
Wedges of Fruit

Method: Heat the honey, lemon juice and butter until blended. Dip wedges of fruit in the sauce and thread alternately on skewers. Barbecue or broil 3″ or 4″ from heat until fruit is glazed and heated through. Turn frequently brushing with remaining sauce to prevent scorching.

Nigel Gordon: The two sauces can be served with ice-cream and the cinnamon butter served on toast, can be eaten for tea in the afternoon.

Barbara Cartland: For boils, carbuncles and other inflamed swellings, Honey taken inside and out will often cure with almost miraculous speed.

Honey Cream Dressing for Fruits

from The Greek Embassy

Ingredients:

2 Eggs
½ cup Honey

$\frac{1}{2}$ cup Lemon Juice
$\frac{1}{4}$ cup Orange Juice
$\frac{1}{2}$ cup Whipped Heavy Cream
2 teasps. Grated Orange Rind
unsweetened Flaked Coconut
$\frac{1}{8}$ teasp. Sea Salt

Method: Beat the eggs in a small saucepan and stir in honey, lemon juice, orange juice and salt. Cook, stirring over a low heat until the mixture coats the back of the spoon. Cool thoroughly. Fold in the cream and orange rind, pour over fresh fruit salad and sprinkle with coconut.

Nigel Gordon: You can also add a selection of mixed nuts to the salad and serve with ice-cream or fresh cream.

Barbara Cartland: When T. M. Davies, the American archaeologist, opened the tomb of Queen Tyi's parents in Egypt, he found a jar of Honey, still in a partly liquid state. Although it had been sealed and placed in the tomb 3,300 years ago the Honey was in perfect condition and delicious to eat.

Honey Nut Sauce

from Canada

Ingredients:

1 tblsp. Coffee
2 tblsps. Water

1 cup Liquid Honey
¼ cup Toasted Almonds

Method: Dissolve the coffee in boiling water. Combine with the honey and almonds.

Butterscotch Sauce

from Gales Honey Bureau

Ingredients:

2 ozs. Butter
6 ozs. Brown Sugar
4 tblsps. Milk
1 tblsp. Honey

Method: Place all the ingredients in a small pan. Cook over gentle heat for 30 minutes until all the sugar has dissolved and the sauce has become dark and thick. Serve this sauce while it is still bubbling.

Nigel Gordon: These two sauces are most delicious on vanilla ice-cream.

Barbara Cartland: Eros tipped his arrows with Honey believing it would spark off true love. The honeymoon as we know it came from an ancient Teutonic Custom. The newly married couple lived on Honey after their wedding until the next full moon. This ensured a large and happy family.

Sweet and Sour Sauce

from Ted Moloney from Australia

Ingredients:

> 1 dstsp. Soy Sauce
> 2 teasps. Cornflour
> 1 cup Vinegar
> 1½ cups Chicken Stock
> ¾ cup Honey
> 1 cup Pineapple Chunks
> 1 small Capsicum

Method: Stir together soy sauce and cornflour and blend vinegar and chicken stock into it. Put mixture in a saucepan and cook over a moderate heat. As it begins to warm, stir in the honey. Follow on with the pineapple chunks and the capsicum which has had the seeds removed, cut into finger size pieces and give a 2 minute boil. Keep over the heat for a few more minutes. You may like a little more sharpness with the vinegar or soy sauce.

Nigel Gordon: This sauce goes with anything like prawns, cold meats, or steamed fresh fish. For the fish steam for a few minutes and flake. Reheat fish in the sauce and serve with boiled rice. Even better use packaged fried rice.

Barbara Cartland: Albert Namagjira is a distinguished Australian aboriginal artist, three of whose pictures were bought by the Queen. He found that eating ordinary European food made him put on so much weight that it affected his health. When he reached 252 lbs. he found it difficult to paint.

He reverted to an aboriginal diet and ate several pounds of Honey almost every day. He lost weight very quickly and his health became strong again.

"I always feel well on my diet of Honey," artist Namagjira explained to his doctor.

COSMETICS

Honey Cosmetics to Make for Yourself

One of the loveliest women in the '20s and '30s was Clare Tennyson at one time the wife of Lord Tennyson, the Captain of England's Cricket XI. Clare Tennyson used to use pure Honey on her beautiful face and when her children were grown up she still looked a girl. There are excellent Honey creams in Health Stores but for those who find it cheaper to make their own here are some recipes.

This is an easy FACE CREAM which will keep a week in the refrigerator—Mix 2 teasps. of Honey with 2 tblsps. of Cream, whisk until fairly thick.

Another FACE CREAM. Mix 2 teasps. of Honey into a well beaten white of egg, add a few drops of almond oil. Mix till a fine smooth cream is formed.

For a quick HONEY HAND CREAM take the white of an egg, a teaspoon of glycerine, and 1 oz. of liquid Honey, and knead them into sufficient barley flour to make a paste.

For a HONEY HAIR TREATMENT mix 4 ozs. of liquid Honey and 4 ozs. of pure olive oil and store away in a warm place. Before you wash your hair, shake the bottle so that the honey and oil mix thoroughly as this will separate when standing. Then massage a generous amount into the hair and continue to work the lotion into the scalp for some minutes.

Warm the head with a hair-dryer. Allow the lotion to remain on for 20 minutes to half an hour, then wash the hair with a herbal shampoo.

This will help to maintain both the colour and healthy lustre of your hair and keep the scalp very clean. This is most effective with brunettes.

DRINKS

Chocolate Milk Drink

Ingredients:

>2 tblsps. Drinking Chocolate
>2 tblsps. Clear Honey
>½ pint Milk

Nigel Gordon: Put the chocolate, honey and milk into the liquidizer until smooth and fluffy. Serve hot or cold.

Honey and Orange

Ingredients:

>½ pint Orange Juice
>1 tblsp. Honey
>2 teasps. Wheat Germ

Nigel Gordon: Stir the honey into the orange juice, add wheat germ and stir. Serve cold or heat but do not boil as you lose the vitamin content from the oranges.

Honey Lemonade

Ingredients:

> 1 cup Honey
> ½ cup Lemon Juice
> 1 quart Water
> Pinch Salt

Nigel Gordon: Mix honey with the water, add lemon juice and salt. Serve hot or cold depending upon the weather.

Fruit Punch

Ingredients:

> 1 cup Honey
> 1½ cups Strong Tea
> 1 cup Orange Juice
> 1 Pint Ginger Ale
> ½ cup Lemon Juice
> 1 cup Fresh Fruit (crushed)
> Pinch Salt

Nigel Gordon: Mix all the ingredients together except the ginger ale. Just before serving add ginger ale and crushed ice. If too strong, weaken with iced water.

Eggnog

Ingredients:

1 Egg
1 teasp. Honey
½ cup Milk
8 teasps. Ground Ginger
⅛ teasp. Cinnamon
2 teasps. Brandy.

Nigel Gordon: Separate egg and beat the white until stiff. Add honey and beat in well. Beat together egg yolk, milk, spices, and brandy. Fold in egg white.

Honey Raspberry Drink

Ingredients:

2 tblsps. Raspberry Juice
1 tblsp. Honey
1 glass Milk

Nigel Gordon: Mix the juice, honey and milk together and dilute with water to taste.

Barbara Cartland: All the time you are drinking these delicious drinks remember that Honey *heals* the windpipe through which you breathe and live, and benefits the soul which gives you immortal life.

THE FASCINATING FORTIES BY BARBARA CARTLAND

'Forty is the youth of old age and the old age of youth' and it is a time when you can combine vitality and beauty with experience and wisdom.

For everyone who believes that to be attractive is the prerogative of youth, here is a book that highlights the triumph of the 'fascinating Forties'. Only with maturity comes charm, poise, glamour, and the spiritual and sexual fulfilment that contribute to the creation of a beautiful woman . . .

Barbara Cartland, playright, lecturer, novelist, T.V. personality and President of the National Association for Health, is a dynamic example of the fact that age sets no limits on beauty, vivacity and style. In THE FASCINATING FORTIES she offers encouragement and down-to-earth practical advice for all those approaching what can be the most exciting period of their lives . . .

0 552 09169 3   30p

A SELECTION OF DIET, HEALTH AND COOKERY BOOKS
PUBLISHED BY CORGI BOOKS

All these books are available at your bookshop or newsagent: or can be ordered direct from the publisher. Just tick the titles you want and fill in the form below.

✦✦

CORGI BOOKS, Cash Sales Department, P.O. Box 11, Falmouth, Cornwall.

Please send cheque or postal order, no currency.
U.K. and Eire send 15p for first book plus 5p per copy for each additional book ordered to a maximum charge of 50p to cover the cost of postage and packing.
Overseas Customers and B.F.P.O. allow 20p for first book and 10p per copy for each additional book.

NAME (Block letters) ....

ADDRESS ....

(DEC. 75) ....

While every effort is made to keep prices low, it is sometimes necessary to increase prices at short notice. Corgi Books reserve the right to show new retail prices on covers which may differ from those previously advertised in the text or elsewhere.